Would You Rather Game Book For Kids 6-12 Years Old

200 Funny Scenarios, Wacky Choices and Hilarious Situations for the Whole Family

With Fun Illustrations

Riddleland

Table of Contents

Introduction

"The important thing is not to stop questioning" ~ Albert Einstein

We would like to personally thank you for purchasing this book. **Would you rather game book for kids 6-12 years old** is a collection of 200 of the funniest scenarios, wacky choices, and hilarious situations for the kids to choose from. It is also fill with fun and cute illustrations.

These questions are an excellent way to get a conversation started in a fun and exciting way. Also, by asking "Why" after a "would you rather question", you may find interesting answers and learn a lot about a person.

We wrote this book because we want children to be encouraged to read more, think and grow. As parents we know that when children play games and learn, they are being educated whilst having so much fun that they don't even realize they're learning and developing valuable life skills.

'Would you Rather ...' is one of our favourite games to play as a family. Some of the 'would you rather ...' scenarios have had us in fits of giggles, others have generated reactions such as: "eeeeeuuugh that's gross!" and yet others still really make us think and reflect and consider our decisions.

Beside have fun, playing the game also has other benefits such as:

- **Communication** – This game helps children to interact, read aloud and listen to others. It's a great way to connect. It's a fun way for parents to get their children interacting with them, without a formal awkward conversation. The game can help to get to know someone better and learn about their likes, dislikes and values.

- **Builds Confidence** – Children get used to pronouncing vocabulary, asking questions and it helps to deal with shyness.

- **Develops Critical Thinking** – It helps children to defend and justify the rationale for their choices and can generate discussions and debates. Parents playing this game with young children, can give them prompting questions about their answers to help them reach logical and sensible decisions.

- **Improves Vocabulary** – Children will be introduced to new words in the questions, and the context of them will help them remember them because the game is fun.

- **Encourages Equality and Diversity** – Considering other people's answers, even if they differ from your own, is important for respect, equality, diversity, tolerance, acceptance and inclusivity. Some questions may get children to think about options available to them, that don't fall into gendered stereotypes, i.e., careers or activities that challenge the norm.

Rules of the Games

This game is probably best played with other people, so if you can, play it with friends or family.

If you have two players

- Player 1 takes the book and ask the player 2 a question beginning with the phrase "Would you rather...? Why?
- After player 2 made his/her choice, he/she would have to explain reason why the choice was made.
- Pass the book to the other player, and they ask you a question.
- Learn lots about one another, have fun and giggles.
- The Two Player game version could work well as an ice-breaker exercise prior to introductions in classes or meetings.

If you have three or four players

- Out of your group decide who will be the question master. If you can't decide, have folded bits of paper with 'Question Master' written on one, and 'players' on the other and each pick one.

- The question Master asks one question from the book.

- The other two or three people give their answers.

- The Question Master decides who has given the best answer – this is the answer with the best explanation for why. The explanations can be funny, or creative or well thought out. The Question Master's decision is final. One point is given for the best answer. If the Question Master can't decide, both players get one point each.

- The first player to reach a score of 10 points wins.

LET THE FUN BEGIN!

Get the Bonus Book!

FUN RIDDLES
AND
silly jokes
— FOR —
KIDS AND FAMILY

*50 bonus
riddles, jokes and funny stories*

RIDDLELAND

https://bit.ly/riddlelandbonusbook

Thank you for buying this book, We would like to share a special bonus as a token of appreciation. It is collection 50 original jokes, riddles and 2 super funny stories!

RIDDLES AND JOKES CONTESTS!!

Riddleland is having **2 contests** to see who is the smartest or funniest boys and girls in the world!

1) **Creative and Challenging Riddles**
2) **Tickle Your Funny Bone Contest**

Parents, please email us your child's "Original" Riddle or Joke **and he or she could win a $50 gift card to Amazon.**

Here are the rules:

1) It must be challenging for the riddles and funny for the jokes!
2) It must be 100% Original and not something from the internet! It is easy to find out!
3) You can submit both joke and riddle as they are 2 separate contests.
4) No help from the parents unless they are as funny as you.
5) Winners will be announced via email.
6) Email us at <u>Riddleland@riddlelandforkids.com</u>

WOULD YOU RATHER....

Eat only with a fork
for the rest of your life
or
only with a spoon?

Lip read

or

be able to understand sign language?

WOULD YOU RATHER....

Have a spinach smoothie for breakfast
each morning
or
eat a lemon each morning?

Eat cold frozen food throughout the
winter

or

very hot food throughout the summer?

WOULD YOU RATHER....

Eat a whole cake
Or
a whole tub of ice-cream dinner every
night for 1 month?

Have a doppelganger who you could send
to activities in your place that you didn't
want to do
or
have the ability to alter people's
memories?

WOULD YOU RATHER....

Find a treasure box full of chocolate

or

gummy bears

Touch a person and this makes them
incapable of lying
or
touch a person and heal whatever is
wrong with them?

WOULD YOU RATHER....

In a fantasy game play a wizard

or

a goblin?

Click your fingers and things you had
lost appear
or
click your fingers to get your bedroom
to tidy itself?

WOULD YOU RATHER....

Be sliding down a water slide
or
climb a climbing frame?

Discover Atlantis

or

Area 51?

WOULD YOU RATHER....

Ride on the back of a camel
or
an elephant?

Try to eat ice-cream that was
catapulted at you

or

have to eat all meals without using your
hands?

WOULD YOU RATHER....

Have the superpower to fly
or
super strength?

Move items with your mind (telekinesis)
or

see anywhere else in the world from
where you are (remote viewing)?

WOULD YOU RATHER....

Go back in time to see dinosaurs
or
cavemen?

Have the ability to time travel in the
future and take a photograph

or

spend an hour with someone who is no
longer living (family or famous)?

WOULD YOU RATHER....

Ride a wild horse that you may fall from
or
get paint splash on your head that stays
forever?

Have bright sunshine all day and night
or
darkness all day and night?

WOULD YOU RATHER....

Would you rather kiss a mouse
or
eat 2 worms?

When you look through your eyes see
everything in cartoon form

or

see everything as it is in reality, but
black and white?

WOULD YOU RATHER....

Be a child your entire life

or

a grown-up your entire life?

Get detention for a whole year
or
never watch TV for 1 year?

WOULD YOU RATHER....

Be in a cage full of snakes
or
full of crocodiles?

When you look through your eyes see
everything in cartoon form

or

see everything as it is in reality, but
black and white?

WOULD YOU RATHER....

Step on a pile of worms
or
step on an ant hill?

Keep a wallet if you found it and spend
the money in it
or
try to find its owner to return it?

WOULD YOU RATHER....

Have a genie grant 3 wishes
or
be lucky for life?

Be able to eat whatever food you want
when you want
or
get to choose what time you go to bed
each night?

WOULD YOU RATHER....

Stay a child until you reached your 70th
birthday
or
instantly be 35 years old?

Be able to make plants grow within
seconds
or
to make it rain when you clap your
hands?

WOULD YOU RATHER....

Communicate with birds
or
with cats?

Never need to get washed but smell nice

Or

never need to go to hairdresser but
keep the same style for the rest of your
life?

WOULD YOU RATHER....

Have a long beard
or
a very hairy body?

Be able to speed-read a book in seconds
and retain the information
or
be able to play back your dreams on your
own personal cinema screen?

WOULD YOU RATHER....

Everything you draw comes to life
or
every story you write to come true?

Be able to never have a bad dream

or

to remember your dreams each morning?

WOULD YOU RATHER....

Be able to feel colours
or
smell sound?

Be able to hold your breath for two
hours
or
be able to transform rice into any food
product?

WOULD YOU RATHER....

Have a bear
or
a lion for a pet?

Juggle eggs over a kitchen floor that
your Mum has just mopped
or
shake a bottle of open ketchup near
some laundry your mum has just
washed?

WOULD YOU RATHER....

Drink of a cup of mud

or

a cup of hot chocolate with red pepper?

Go back in time to meet up with loved ones who have passed away

or

go to the future to meet up with your children or grandchildren?

WOULD YOU RATHER....

Have a billion dollars that you can spend on anything you want

or

have $1,000 dollars to give to each hungry or homeless person?

Have children aged 19
Or
aged 40?

WOULD YOU RATHER....

Eat a spinach chocolate cake
or
a garlic and onion cupcake?

Would you rather be stuck outside
under a snowstorm

or

a thunderstorm?

WOULD YOU RATHER....

Get sting by bee every month

or

a mosquito every day for a year?

Have the ability to press a button that
stops your Mum
or
your Dad
from talking for one hour?

WOULD YOU RATHER....

Be able to play perfectly every musical instrument you pick up
or
be able to do any style of dancing?

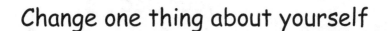

Change one thing about yourself

or

change one thing about your Mum or Dad?

WOULD YOU RATHER....

Get your best friend an expensive gift
or
your parents a very expensive gift?

Have one day where you swapped roles
with your mum or dad and they went to
school and you went to work
or
have one day where your parents were
the same age as you and hung around
with your friends?

WOULD YOU RATHER....

Wear a new pair of sneakers

or

new clothes every week?

Tell your mom

or

dad

what do to for a whole day?

WOULD YOU RATHER....

Be Wonder Woman for month
Or
Batgirl for a year?

Own a fantastic tent with multiple
rooms and modern facilities
or
have a huge TV in your bedroom with
games consoles?

WOULD YOU RATHER....

Be a science teacher
or
a doctor

Know how to code in 5 different
programming languages

or

be able to speak Russian, English,
Chinese, Japanese and Arabic?

WOULD YOU RATHER....

Get an A+ grade on every school exam
or
win every sports game at school?

Travel to every country in the world

or

be able to run a marathon without being tired?

WOULD YOU RATHER....

Go to school wearing a red clown's nose
or
wearing a big blue curly clown's wig?

Have the floors of your house bouncy
like a trampoline

or

the floors heat sensitive so they're
warm on a cold day and cool on a warm
day?

WOULD YOU RATHER....

Have a pet mouse the size of an elephant
or
a little tiny elephant the size of a mouse?

Have the ability to shrink things
or
increase their size?

WOULD YOU RATHER....

Kiss a frog
or
cuddle a tarantula?

Clean up your room every day and do homework only once a week

or

do homework every day and only clean your room once a month?

WOULD YOU RATHER....

Own a dragon
or
a unicorn?

Go to the dentist for a filling

or

the doctor for a shot?

WOULD YOU RATHER....

Have a pet Lion

or

a pet Tiger?

Have gills to breathe under water

or

be able to run across the top of oceans,
seas and lakes?

WOULD YOU RATHER....

Announce to everyone around you
whenever you have to fart
or
poop?

Have the ability to shrink things

or

increase their size?

WOULD YOU RATHER....

Have talking fish
or
a fish that can walk on land?

Be a superhero who has never reveal
your identity

or

a supervillain whom everyone knows you?

WOULD YOU RATHER....

Turn into a magical unicorn
or
a mermaid?

Feel the force of Thor's hammer

or

meet the Hulk when he's angry?

WOULD YOU RATHER....

Start every sentence with, "Hey smelly"
or
end every sentence with "... oopsy daisy"?

Have the power to change your colour like a chameleon (blend into any background)
or
have the ability to shape-shift (imitate anything or person)?

WOULD YOU RATHER....

Get a puppy
or
a new toy every month?

Teleport to any location
or
change into a monster when you're
angry?

WOULD YOU RATHER....

Never eat candy
or
never drink soda for the rest your life?

Have a garden with a dinosaur living in it
or
a large lake with the Loch Ness Monster
in it?

WOULD YOU RATHER....

Eat garlic ice cream
or
onion marshmallow?

Have your friends read your diary
or
do the chicken every time you greet
your friends?

WOULD YOU RATHER....

Have an eagle's eye
or
a beaver's teeth?

Laugh out loud when somebody farted

or

everyone laughing at you when you
farted?

WOULD YOU RATHER....

Hop like a kangaroo
or
walk sideways like a crab?

Go to bed one hour earlier than you
need
or

take a cold shower every morning?

WOULD YOU RATHER....

Live in a pig sty
or
a chicken coop?

Be super fast

or

be able turn into any animal

WOULD YOU RATHER....

Not eat waffles
or
pancakes with syrup again?

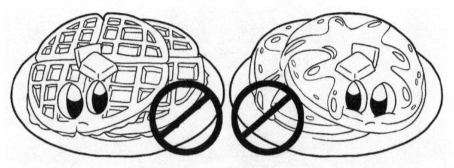

Get to eat meat but have to hunt for
yourself

or

be vegetarian but have to plant for
yourself?

WOULD YOU RATHER....

Go a year without macaroni and cheese
or
pizza?

Sound like Donald Duck
or
Goofy for the rest of your life?

WOULD YOU RATHER....

Eat only broccoli
or
green peas for a whole year?

Burp every time you start a sentence
or
sneeze every time you end a sentence?

WOULD YOU RATHER....

Rain jelly beans
or
snow cotton candy?

Toilet water

or

rotten egg poured on your head?

WOULD YOU RATHER....

Stand up to eat for every meal
or
lie down to drink water?

Be a famous singer

or

a famous actor/actress?

WOULD YOU RATHER....

Spend a day swimming with dolphins

or

climbing trees with monkeys?

Be very famous for something silly
or
have excellent talent but not famous?

WOULD YOU RATHER....

Eat spaghetti without any utensils
or
drink soup with a fork?

Not able to taste anything

or

see everything in black and white?

WOULD YOU RATHER....

Have a hippo-sized cat

or

cat-sized hippo?

Spend an hour with 10 kittens
or
10 puppies?

WOULD YOU RATHER....

Live on a hot air balloon

or

a submarine for a whole summer?

Never have to sit another test or exam at school

or

never catch a cold or stomach bug ever again?

WOULD YOU RATHER....

Have big tiger paws
or
an elephant trunk?

Get to miss one school class each day
and spend time as you want watching TV
or
playing on the computer when you got
home from school?

WOULD YOU RATHER....

Live in the Mars
or
Jupiter for 10 years?

Be able to read an entire book in a
couple of minutes

or

write an essay in your sleep?

WOULD YOU RATHER....

Turn into Hulk when are you are angry
or
being able to lift Thor's hammer?

Attend six classes with your favourite
teacher
or
two with your least favourite teacher?

WOULD YOU RATHER....

Be able to shapeshift into an Eagle so you can fly high in the sky
or
into a whale so you can dive deep in to the ocean?

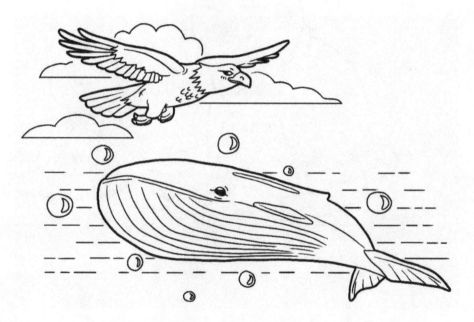

Be a stealth like a ninja
or
graceful like a ballet dancer?

WOULD YOU RATHER....

Have thick fur like a polar bear
or
furless like a Siamese cat?

Be able to play any instrument
or
be able to copy anybody's voice

WOULD YOU RATHER....

Ride on a space rocket
or
hover craft?

Have a dog that behaves like a squirrel

or

a squirrel that behaves like a dog?

WOULD YOU RATHER....

Eat bread
or
rice for every meal for a whole month?

Be one of Santa's workshop elves
or
be the Tooth Fairy's assistant?

WOULD YOU RATHER....

Be an astronaut
or
a deep sea diver?

Have a snowball fight in winter
or
a water balloon fight in summer?

WOULD YOU RATHER....

Be a centaur
or
a minotaur?

Be able to remember all the names of
the people you talked to

or

remember everything in every book you
read?

WOULD YOU RATHER....

Be the king of the Jungle – the Majestic
Lion King
or
King of the Sea – The Ferocious Great
White Shark?

Travel to planet in the solar system
or
every country in the world

WOULD YOU RATHER....

Eat watermelon that taste like
cantaloupe
or
cantaloupe that taste like a strawberry?

Be a singer in an Opera
or
a dancer in a Broadway?

WOULD YOU RATHER....

Eat Bacon caramel chocolate sundae
or
a peanut butter cheese cupcake with
gummi bears

Mow the lawn on a hot summer day
or
shovel snow on a cold winter day?

WOULD YOU RATHER....

Experience a tornado
or
a hurricane?

To have a vision as far as telescope

or

super hearing like superman?

WOULD YOU RATHER....

Walk through slushy snow
or
heavy rain?

Do cartwheels when you want to walk

or

front flips when you want to run?

WOULD YOU RATHER....

Meow like a kitten
or
bark like a dog when you are laughing?

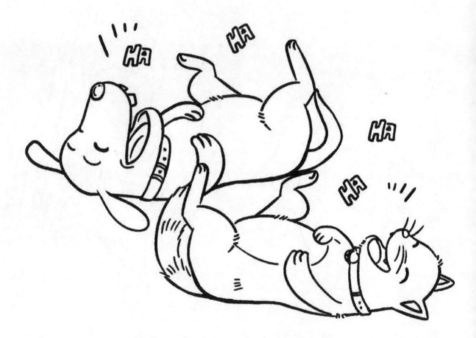

Live in a castle
or
a penthouse suite with amazing views of
the city below?

WOULD YOU RATHER....

Get 1 big present
or
10 small presents for Christmas?

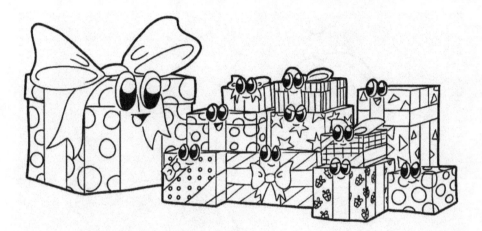

Live in an area with no nearby
neighbours
or
live in a place with many people nearby?

WOULD YOU RATHER....

Live on a spaceship
or
a dessert island?

Inherit your Dad's worst habit

or

your Mum's?

WOULD YOU RATHER....

Wake up early in the morning
or
stay up late at night?

Live like royalty but have no friends

or

live like a homeless person with your
friends and family?

WOULD YOU RATHER....

Own a yacht
or
an island?

Stay up all night helping an irritating member of your family with a problem
or
babysit a baby that screams and cries the whole time?

WOULD YOU RATHER....

Not be able to use your mobile
or
laptop for a year?

Have a bank account that doubles any
money you deposit
or
find $5 under your pillow each morning
when you wake up?

WOULD YOU RATHER....

Give up your TV
or
music for a year?

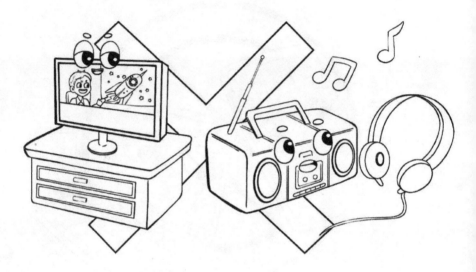

Be correct any time you made a bet

or

know if someone is lying to you?

WOULD YOU RATHER....

Be able to draw anything well
or
play the piano beautifully?

Have only one normal sized hand
or
three tiny hands?

WOULD YOU RATHER....

Go sky diving
or
bungee jumping?

Have a lifetime's supply of chocolate
or
a popular well-known chocolate bar
named after you?

WOULD YOU RATHER....

Be able to play the guitar
or
the violin?

Eat mango ice cream

or

a peach cobbler?

WOULD YOU RATHER....

Face a dragon

or

a phoenix?

Have 100 good friends

or

10 best friends?

WOULD YOU RATHER....

Live in castle

or

in a wooden cabin?

Live to 100 years old

or

be turned into a cyborg so you can live forever?

WOULD YOU RATHER....

Take a bite out of lime

or

a lemon?

Be a policeman
or
a fire fighter?

WOULD YOU RATHER....

Have a treehouse
or
a trampoline in your backyard?

Run without ever feeling tired
or
go for 1 week without sleeping?

WOULD YOU RATHER....

Be chased by a moose
or
a mountain goat?

Visit an aquarium

or

zoo?

WOULD YOU RATHER....

Eat baby back ribs every morning
or
pancakes with syrup every night?

Never play video games
or
never get sick again?

WOULD YOU RATHER....

Ride on a zebra
or
a giraffe?

Learn how to snow ski
or
water ski?

WOULD YOU RATHER....

Wash your hair once a month
or
brush your teeth once a month?

Make a speech

or

dance in front of a thousand people?

WOULD YOU RATHER....

Eat cereal
or
waffle for every meal for a whole week?

Read minds

or

know about the future?

WOULD YOU RATHER....

Learn how to fish
or
how to hunt?

Forget who you were
or
who everyone else was?

WOULD YOU RATHER....

Learn how to juggle 5 balls
or
how to ride on a unicycle?

Feel like you always have to sneeze

or

have everything you touch tickle?

WOULD YOU RATHER....

Be able to go through wall
or
turn invisible?

See everything upside down

or

hear everything backwards?

WOULD YOU RATHER....

Eat rotten vegetables
or
rotten bread?

Be given $500
or
have $1000 donated to charity

WOULD YOU RATHER....

Eat a whole jar of strawberry jam

or

drink a cup of hot sauce?

Have a bottle stuck to each finger on

Or

a bucket stuck to one foot?

WOULD YOU RATHER....

Jump into a pool of chocolate pudding
or
into a pool of blueberry ice cream?

Communicate in sign language

or

through drawing a sketch?

WOULD YOU RATHER....

Eat a can of cat food
or
piece of raw fish?

Always laugh in inappropriate situations
or
never laugh again?

WOULD YOU RATHER....

Have low pitch voice like a gorilla
or
a high pitch voice like a baby?

Be trap in a room with a hungry leopard
or
20 crying babies?

WOULD YOU RATHER....

Brush your teeth with hot sauce
or
mayonnaise?

Have eyes at the back of your head
or
on your hands?

WOULD YOU RATHER....

Have all your clothes be checkered
or
polka dots?

Meet your great grandparents

or your

future great grandchildren?

WOULD YOU RATHER....

Be a snake
or
a scorpion?

Eat pineapple that taste like peach
or
a watermelon taste like carrots?

WOULD YOU RATHER....

Meet a fairy
or
an elf?

Have power to control the weather
or

power to change the past?

One Final Thing...

Thank for making it through to the end of *Would Your Rather...*, *Game Book for Kids 6-12 Years Old*, let's hope it was fun, silly and able to provide you and your family with all of the entertainment you needed for this rainy day (or sunny afternoon)!

Did You Enjoy the Book?

If you did, please let us know by leaving a review on AMAZON. Review let Amazon know that we are creating quality material for children. Even a few words and ratings would go a long way. We would like to thank you in advance for your time.

If you have any comments, or suggestions for improvement for other books, we would love to hear from and you and can contact us at riddleland@riddlelandforkids.com
Your comments are greatly valued, and the book have already been revised and improved as a result of helpful suggestions from readers.

Other Fun Children Books for The Kids!
Riddles Series

Encourage your kids to think outside of the box with these Fun and Creative Riddles!

Get them on Amazon

Try Not to Laugh Challenge Series

Get them on Amazon
or our website at
www.riddlelandforkids.com

Get the Bonus Book!

FUN RIDDLES
AND
silly jokes
— FOR —
KIDS AND FAMILY

50 bonus
riddles, jokes and funny stories

RIDDLELAND

https://bit.ly/riddlelandbonusbook

Thank you for buying this book, We would like to share a special bonus as a token of appreciation. It is collection 50 original jokes, riddles and 2 funny stories

RIDDLES AND JOKES CONTESTS!!

Riddleland is having **2 contests** to see who is the smartest or funniest boys and girls in the world:

1) Creative and Challenging Riddles

2) Tickle Your Funny Bone Contest

Parents, please email us your child's "Original" Riddle or Joke **and he or she could win a $50 gift card to Amazon.**

Here are the rules:

1) It must be challenging for the riddles and funny for the jokes!

2) It must be 100% Original and not something from the internet! It is easy to find out!

3) You can submit both joke and riddle as they are 2 separate contests.

4) No help from the parents unless they are as funny as you.

5) Winners will be announced via email.

6) Email us at <u>Riddleland@riddlelandforkids.com</u>

About the Author

Riddleland is a mom + dad run publishing company. We are passionate about creating fun and innovative books to help children develop their reading skill and fall in love with reading. If you have suggestions for us or want to work with us, shoot us an email at riddleland@riddlelandforkids.com

Our favorite family quote

"Creativity is area in which younger people have a tremendous *advantage since they have an endearing habit of always questioning past wisdom and authority." - Bill Hewlett*

CPSIA information can be obtained
at www.ICGtesting.com
Printed in the USA
BVHW031723180320
575351BV00001B/128